Antique Bird Art 1
- An Adult Coloring Book -

What makes our books unique and different than all the others?

We're the only adult coloring book publisher who uses original antique botanical art in our books. Over the years we've acquired an extensive collection of antique images that we're excited to share with you.

Want to refer to the original art for coloration? If you'd like to see the original art before our conversion to black and white, visit the Book Images section of our website at http://www.BotanicalArtDesigns.com and click on the cover image of your book. You'll be presented with a PDF of the original color images (in as found condition) to use as references as you color.

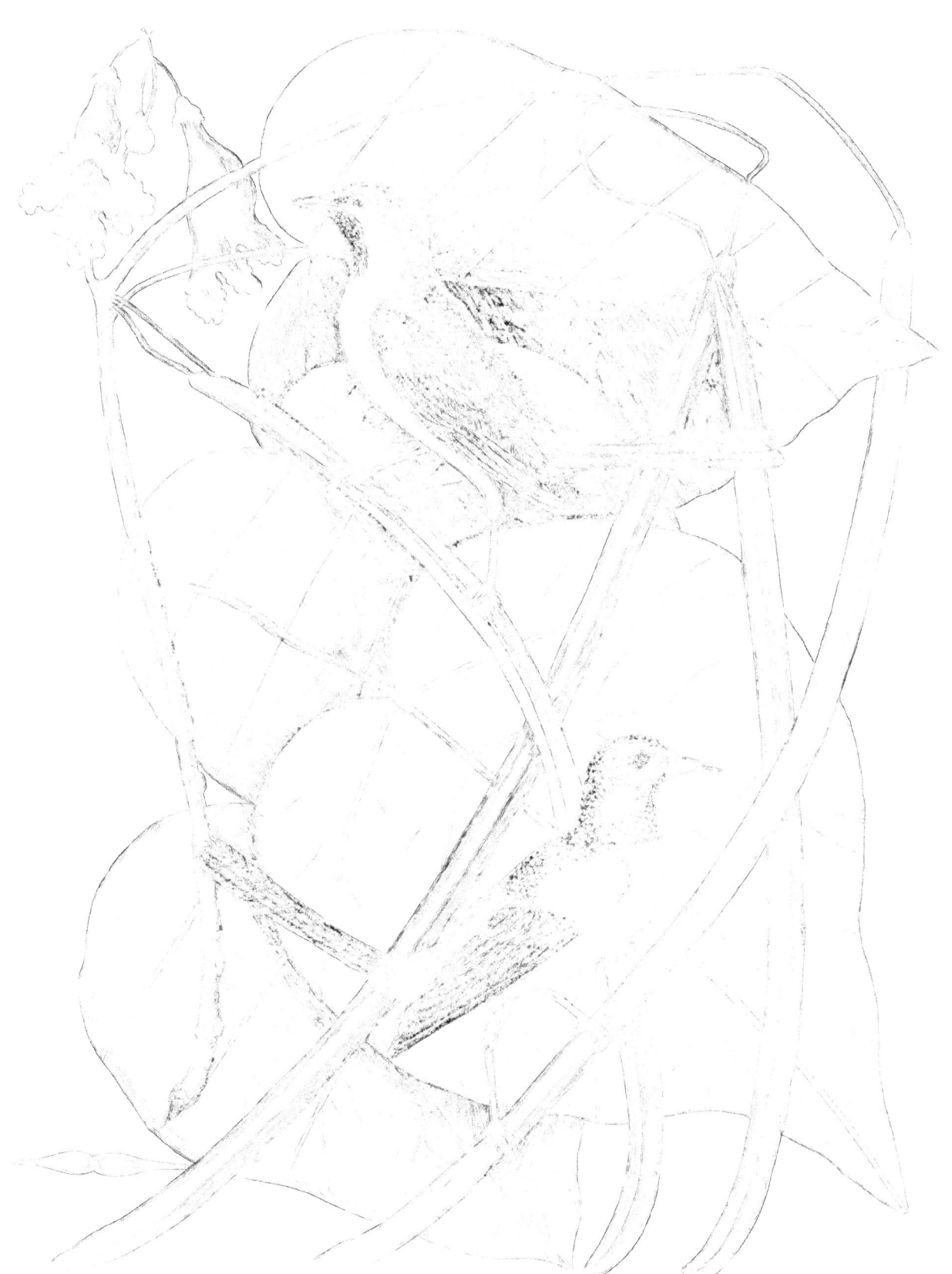

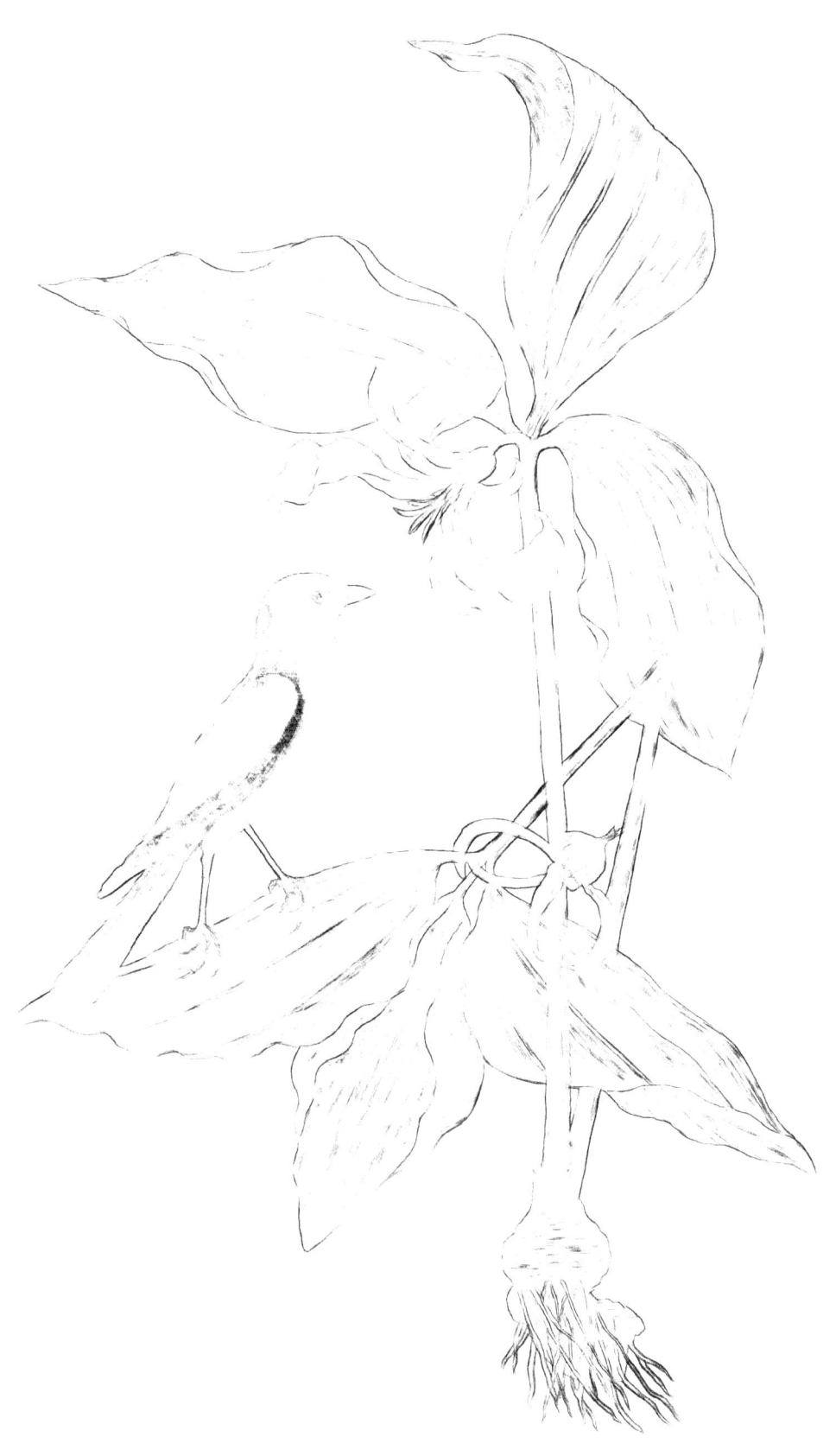

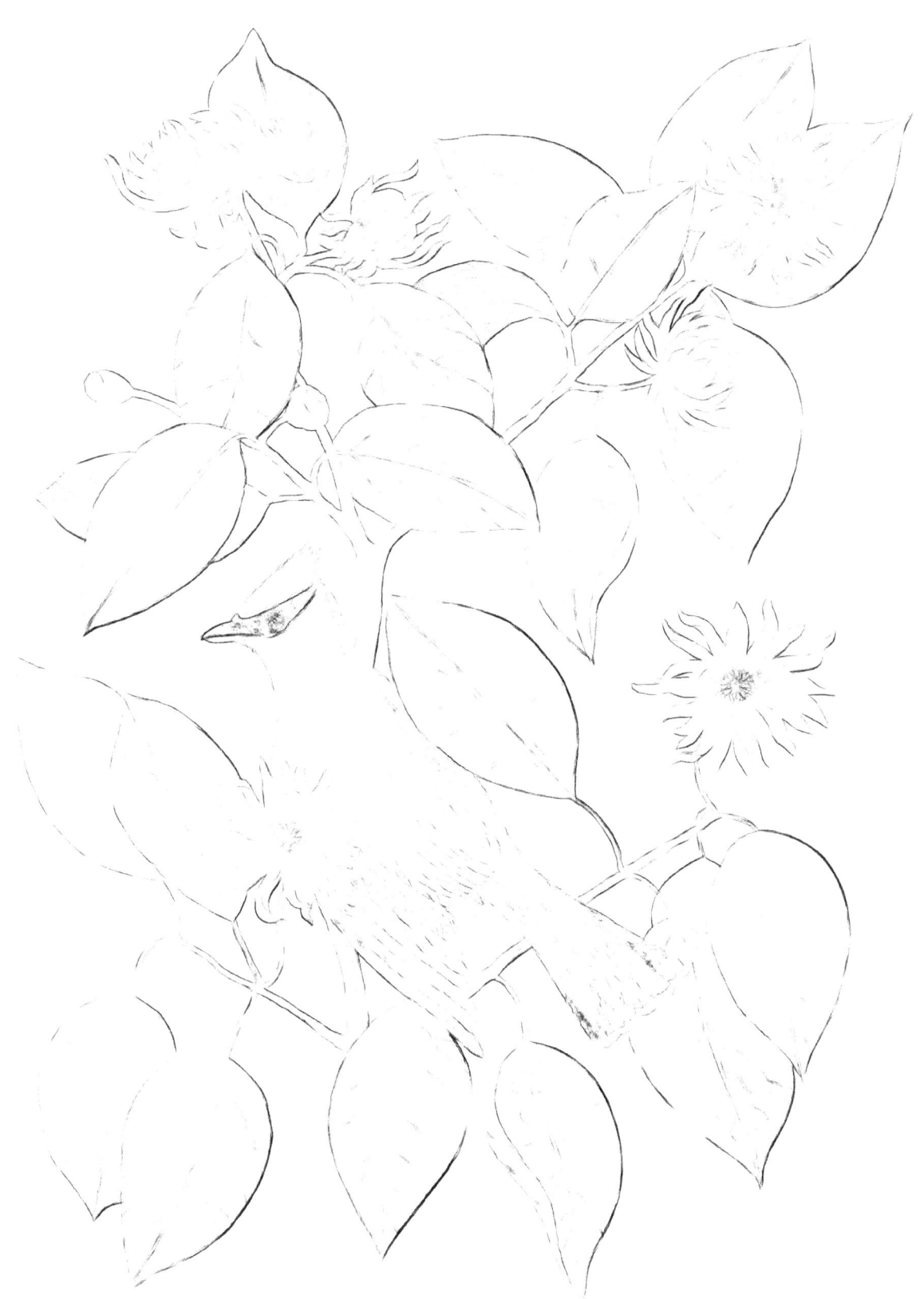

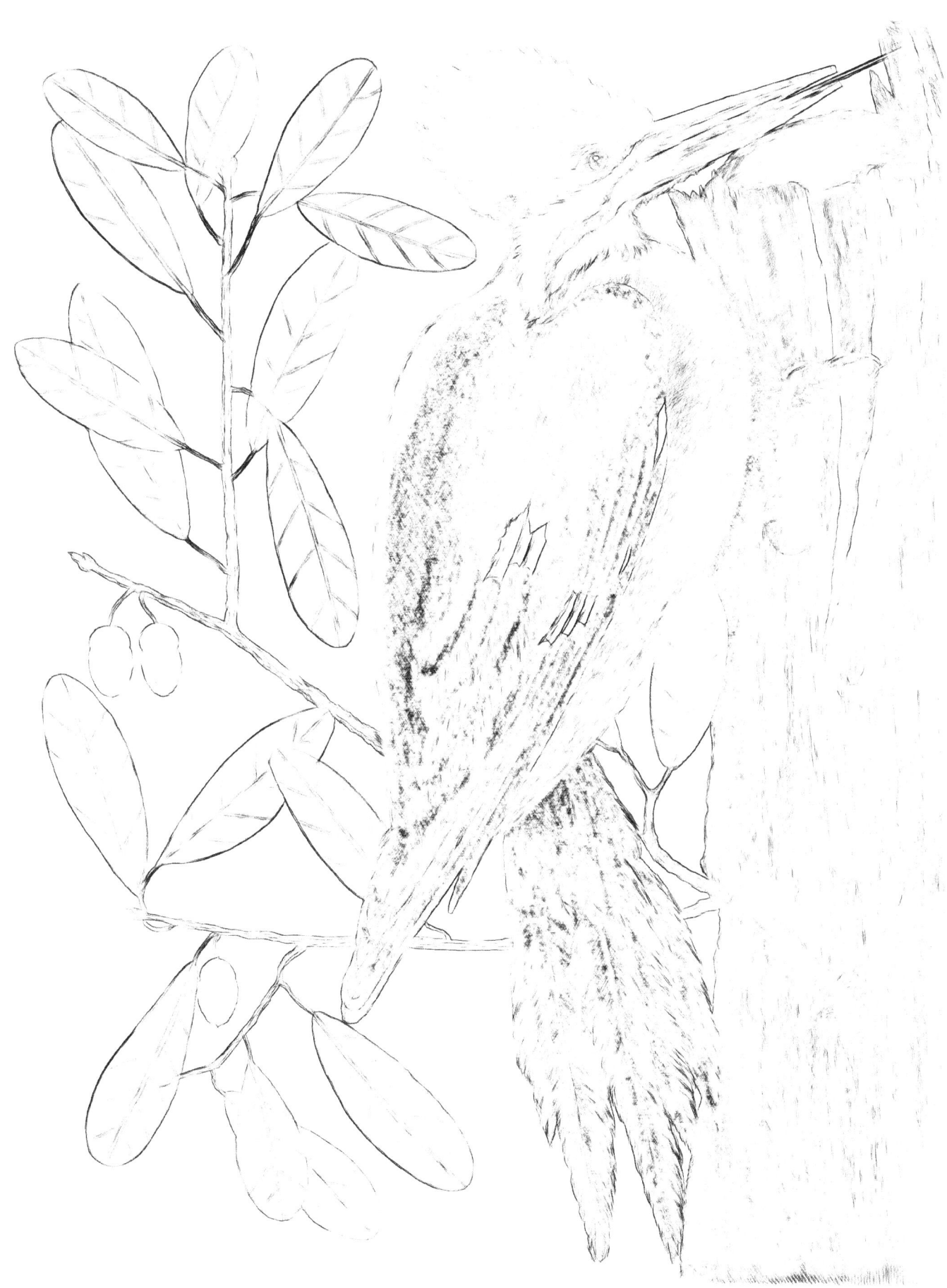

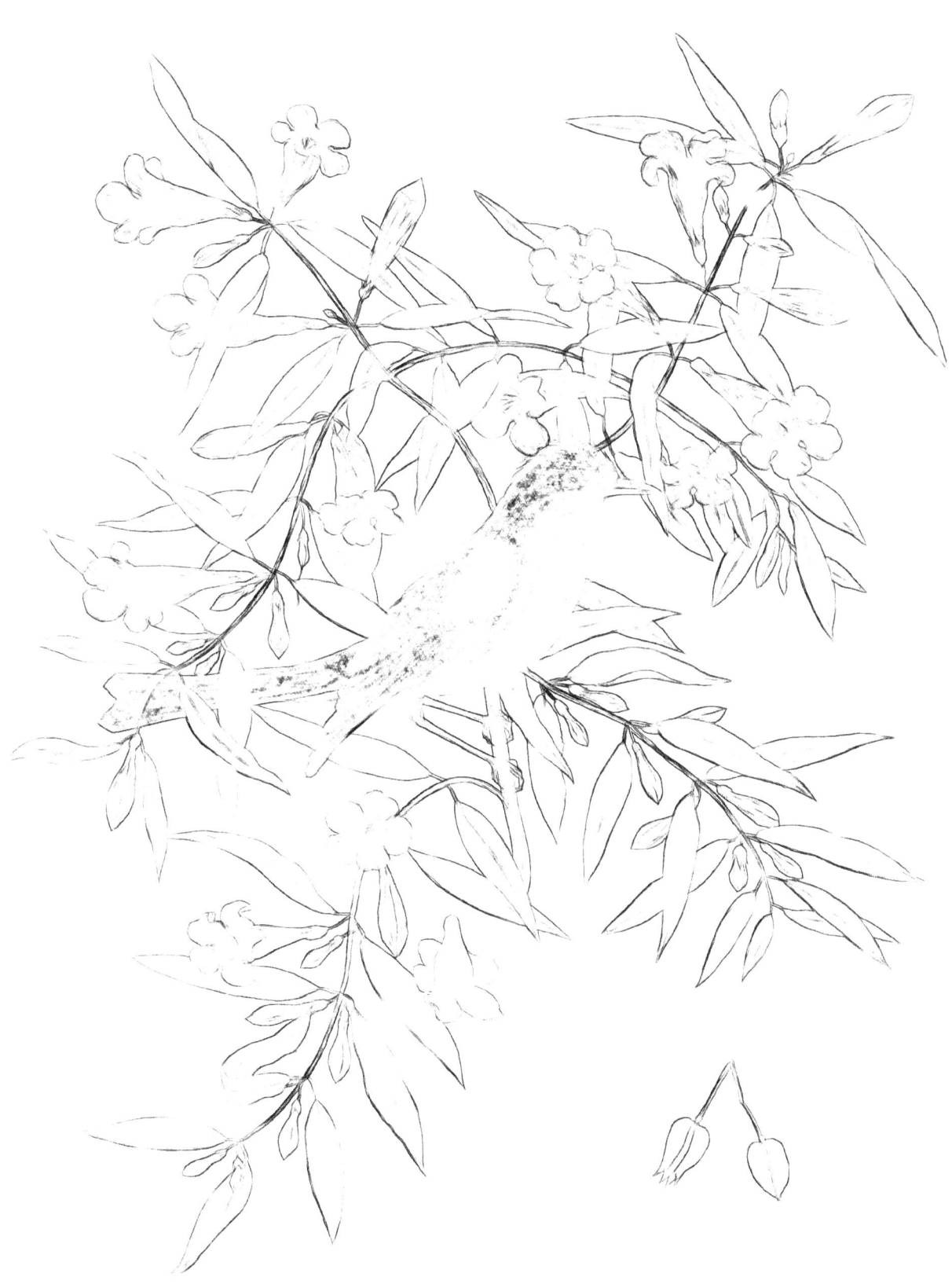

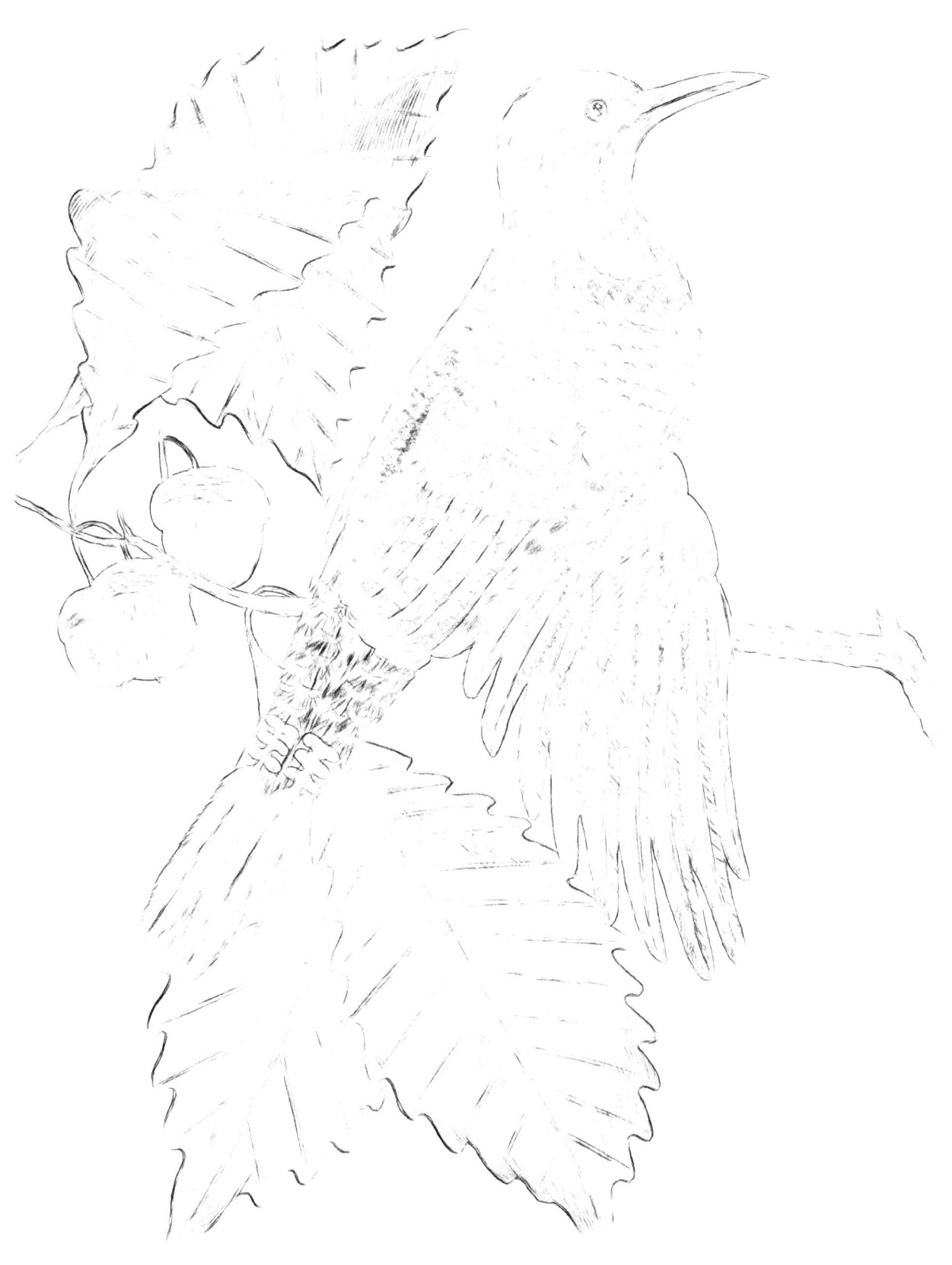

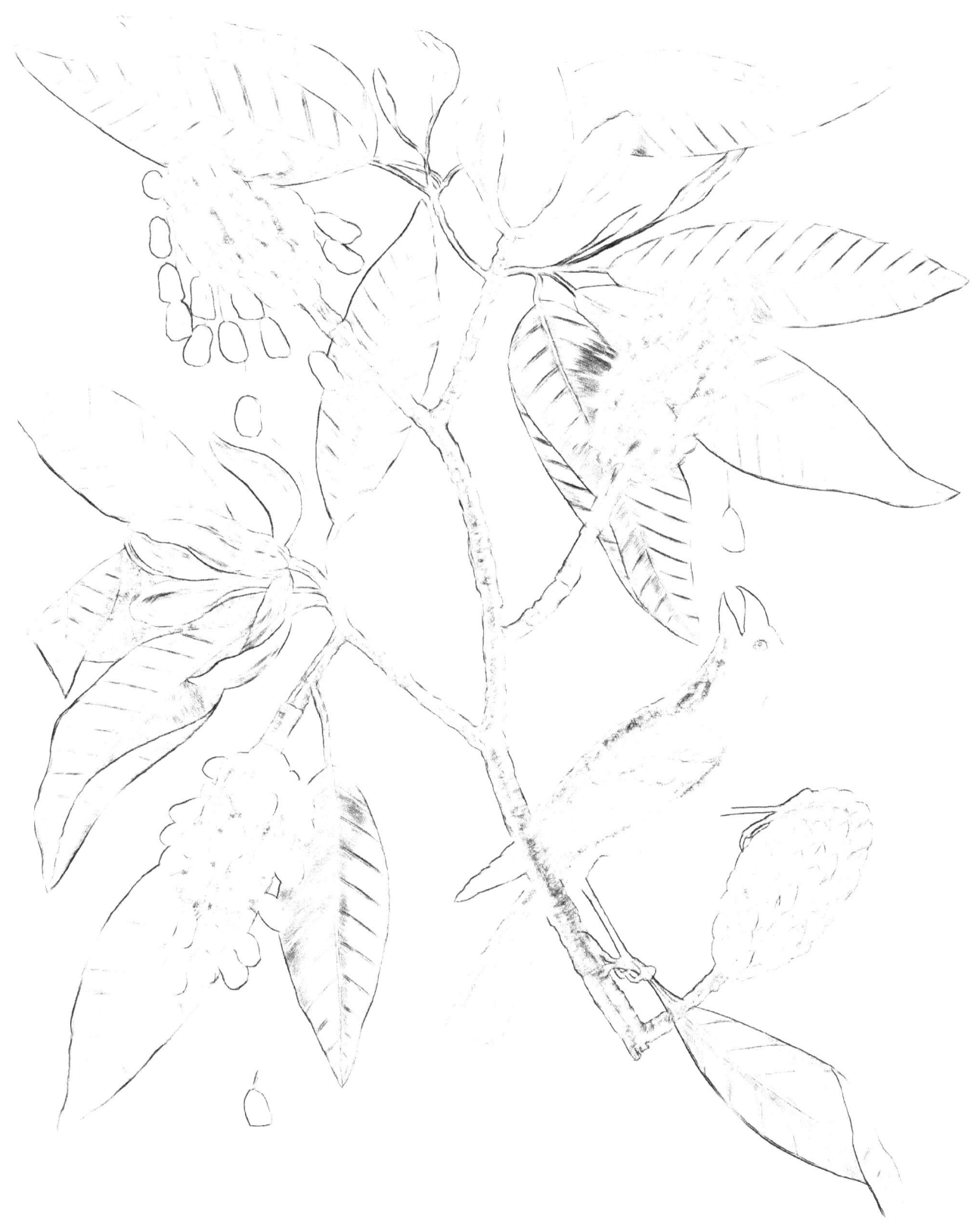

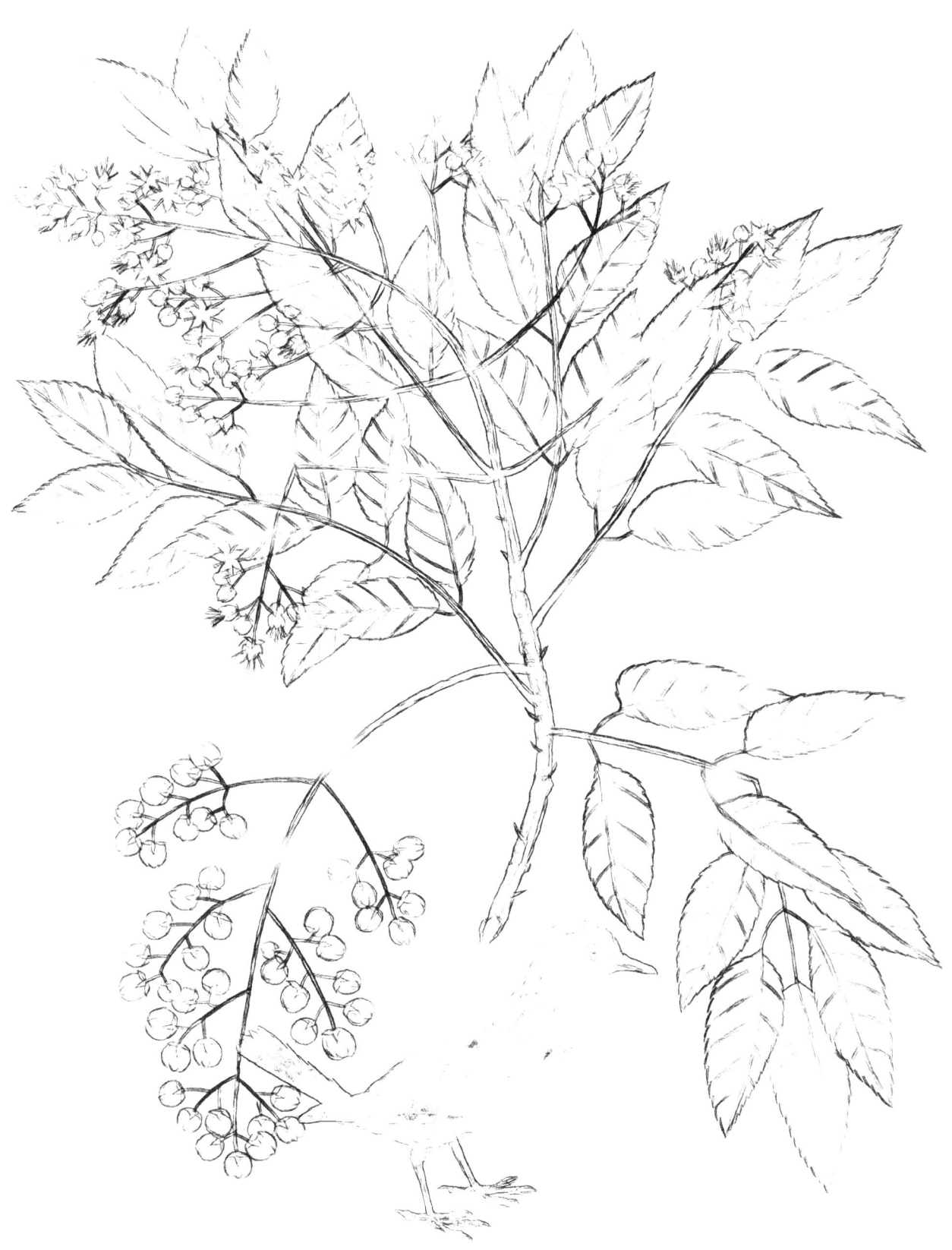

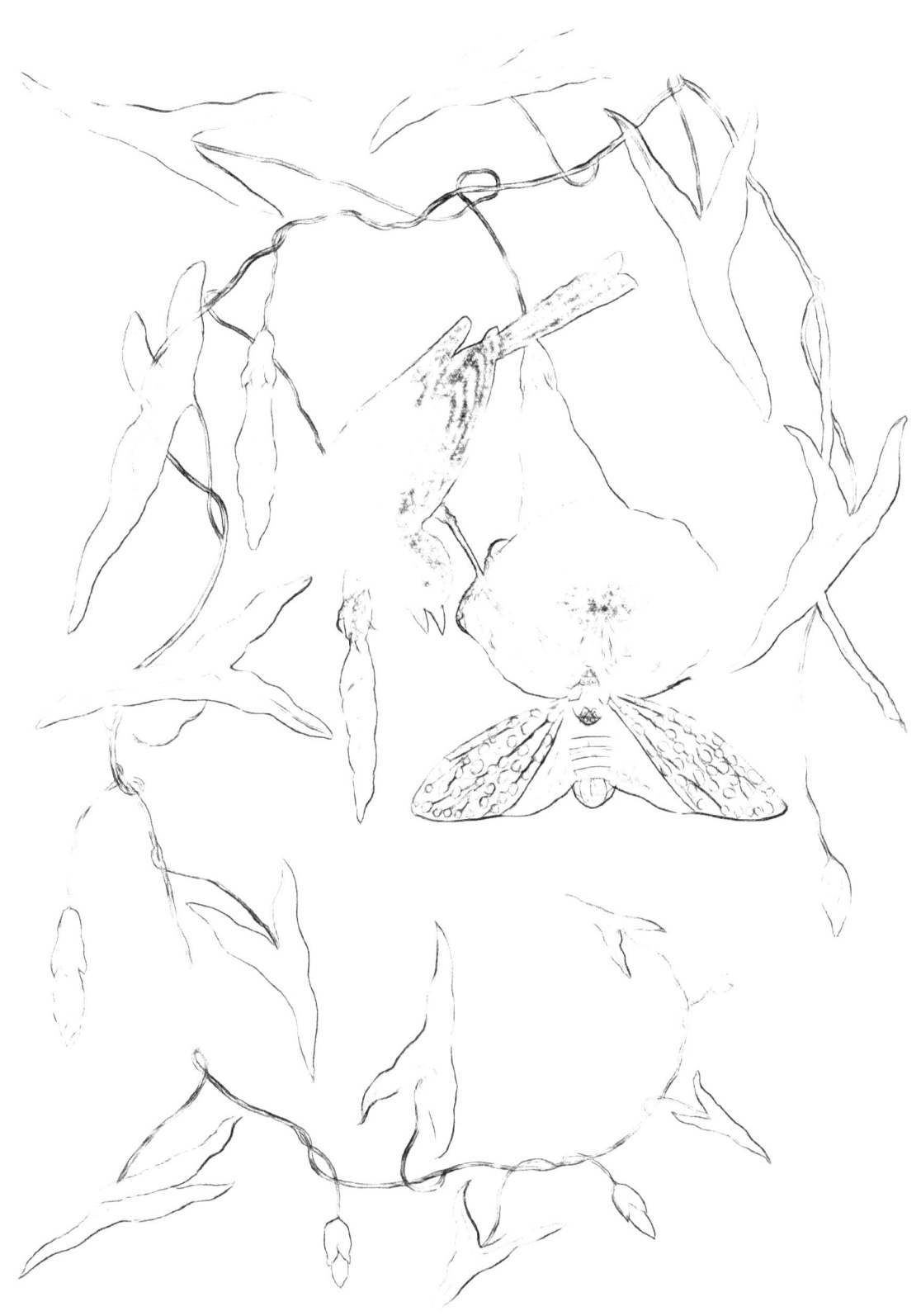

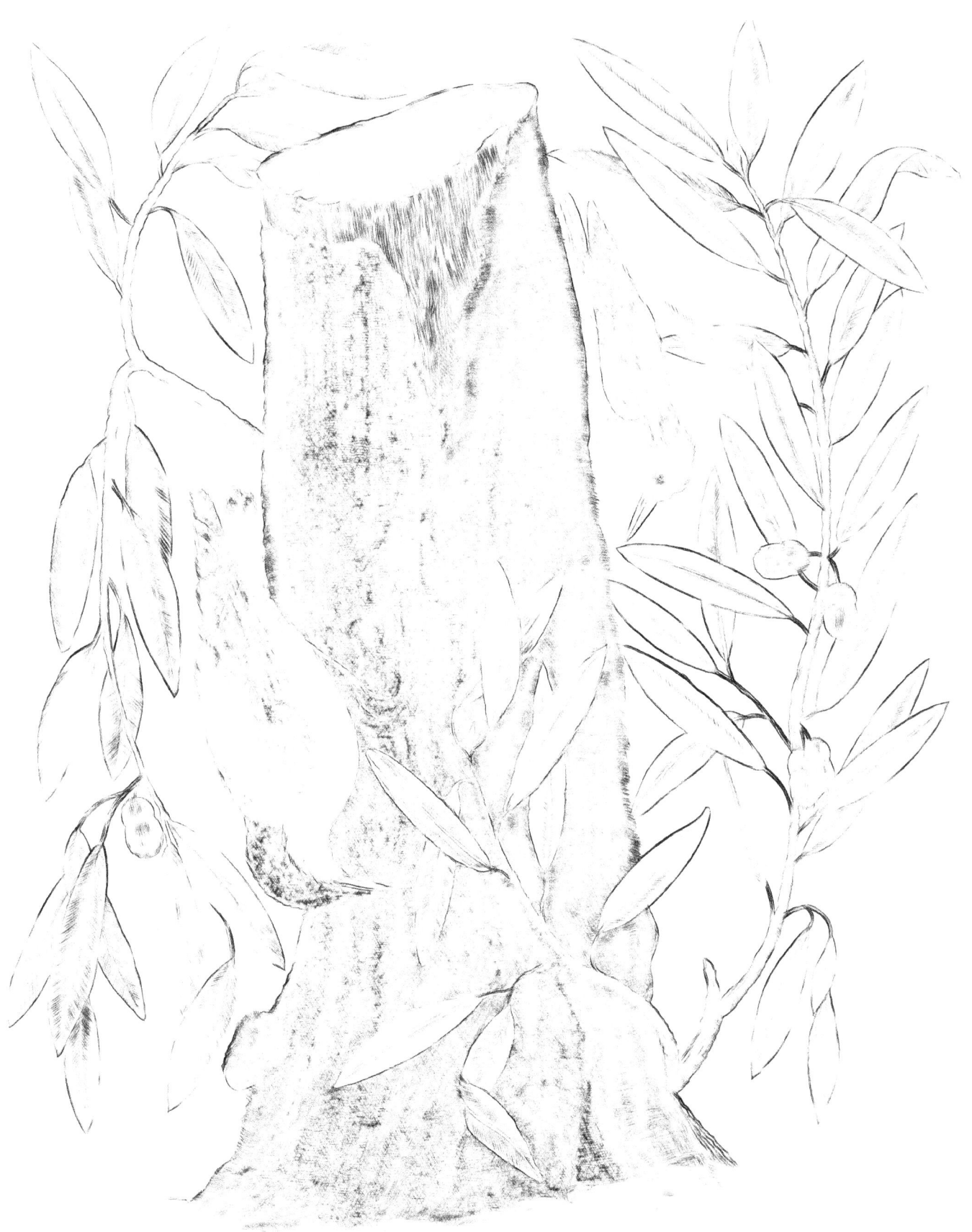

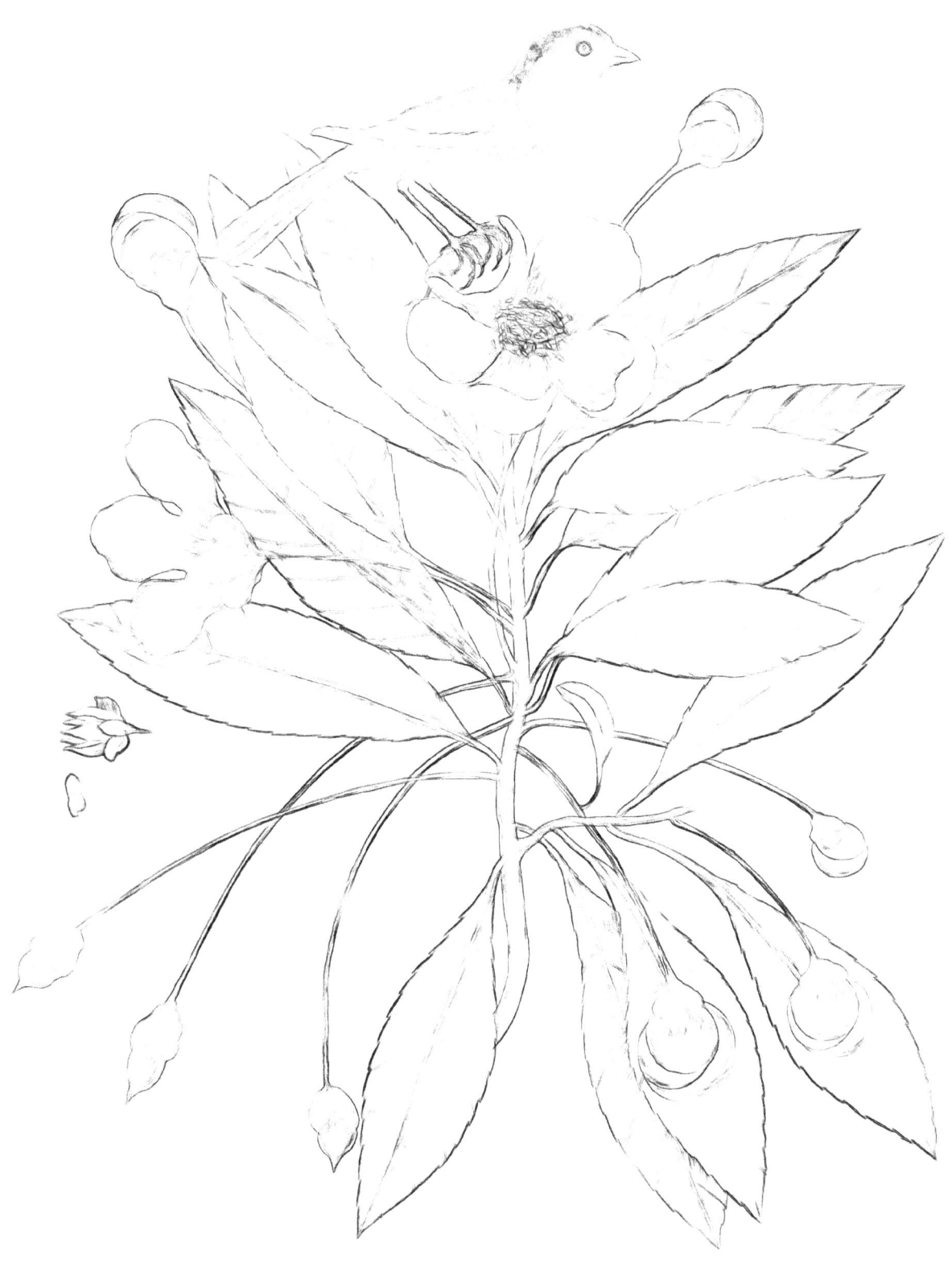

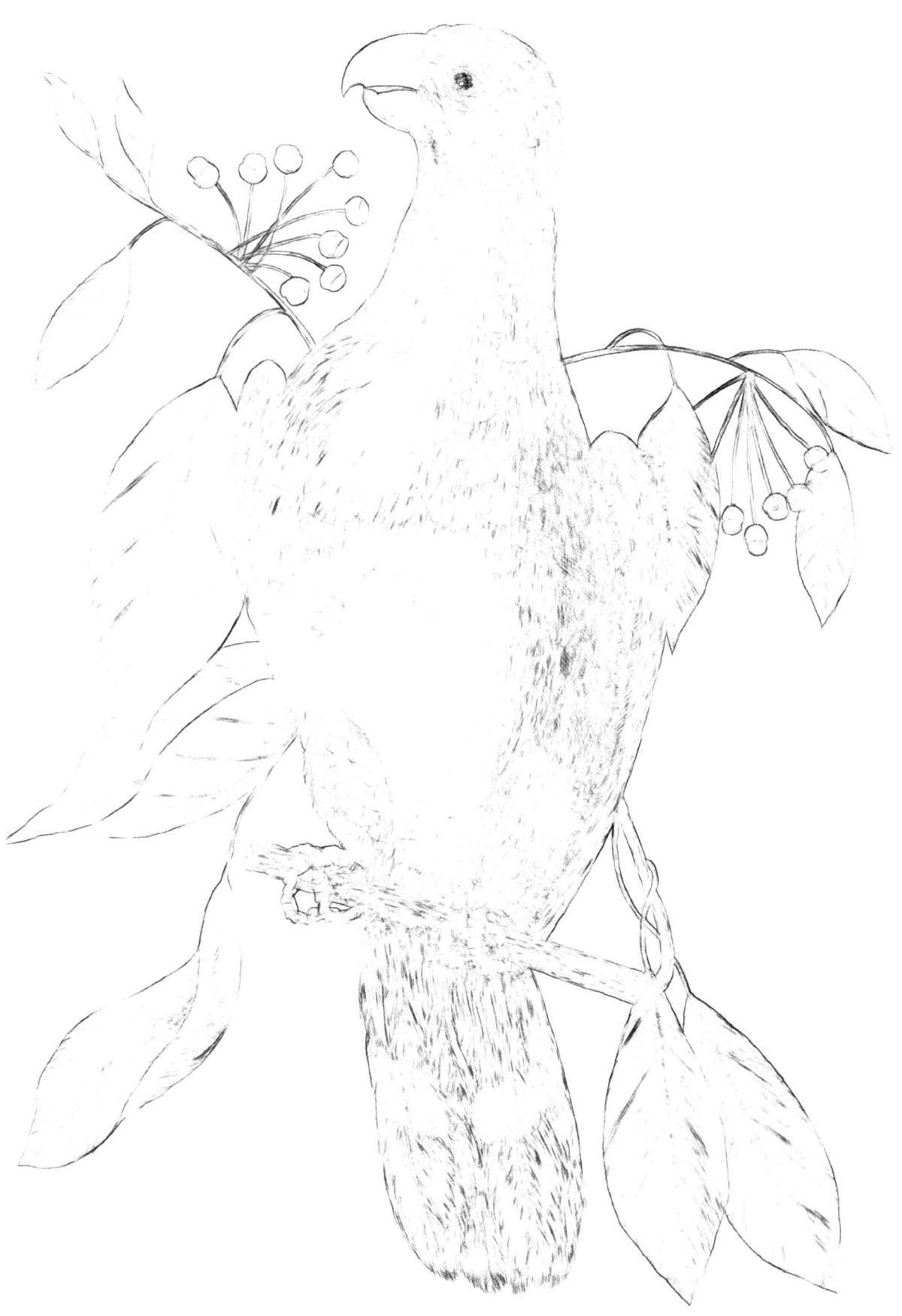

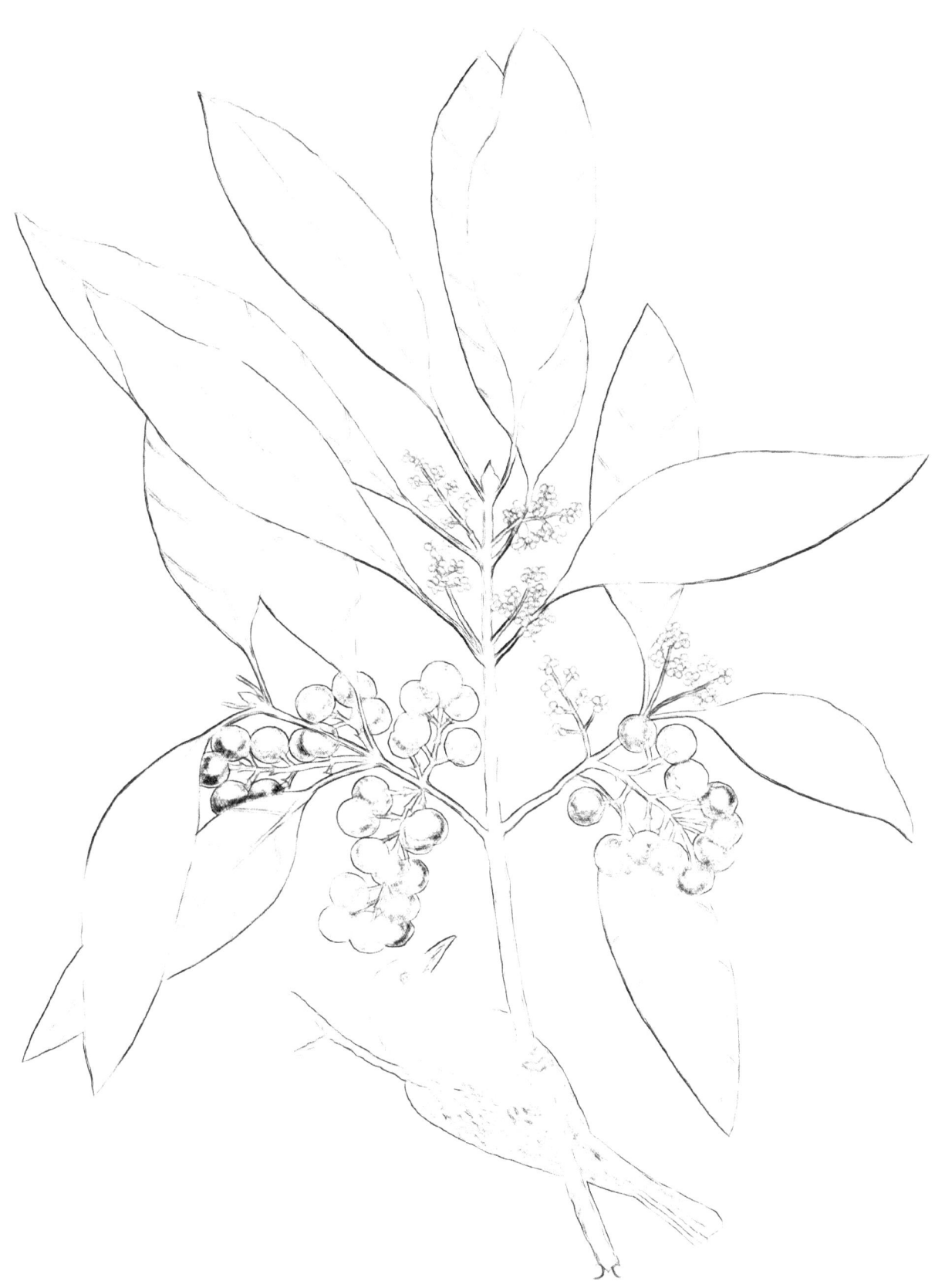

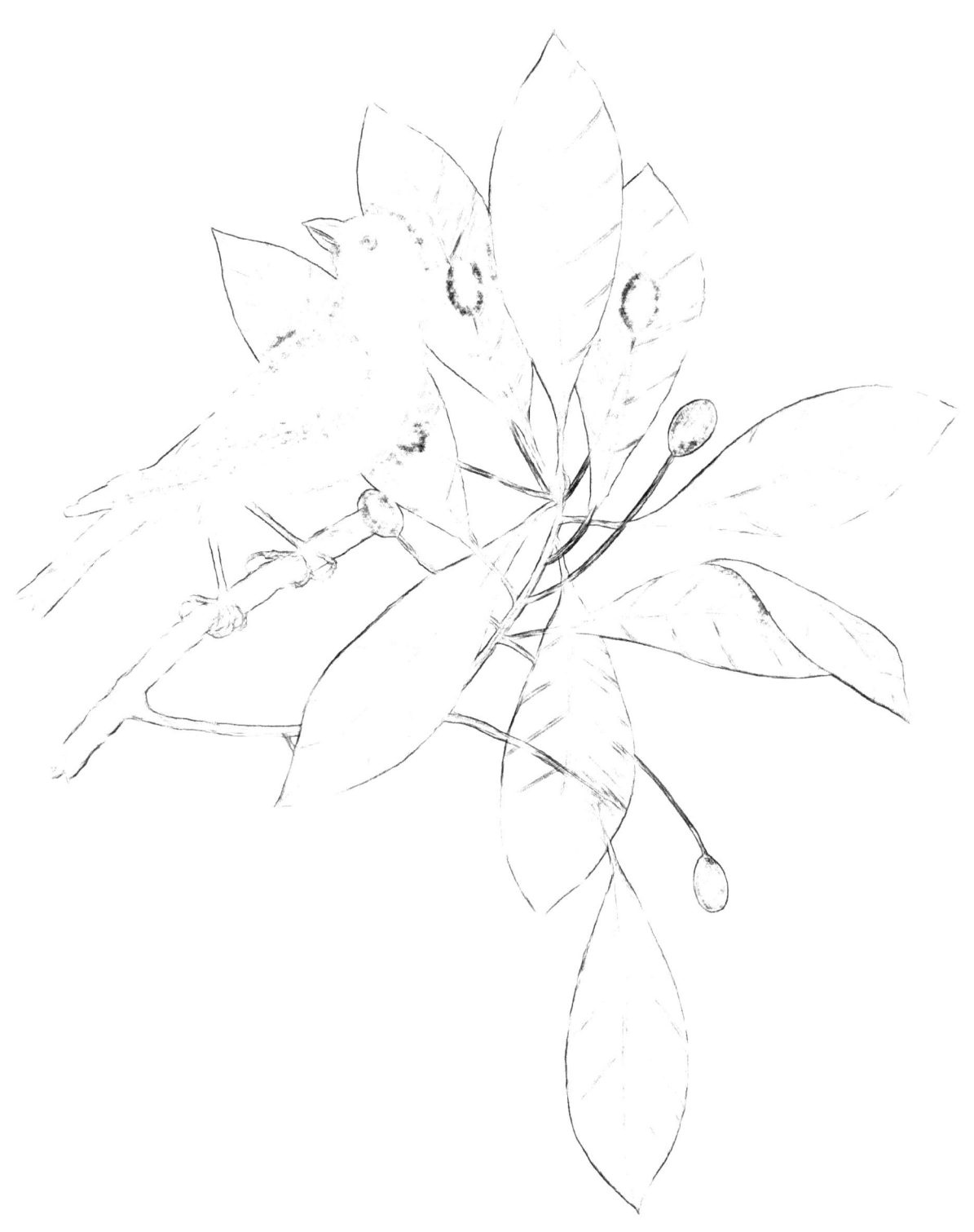

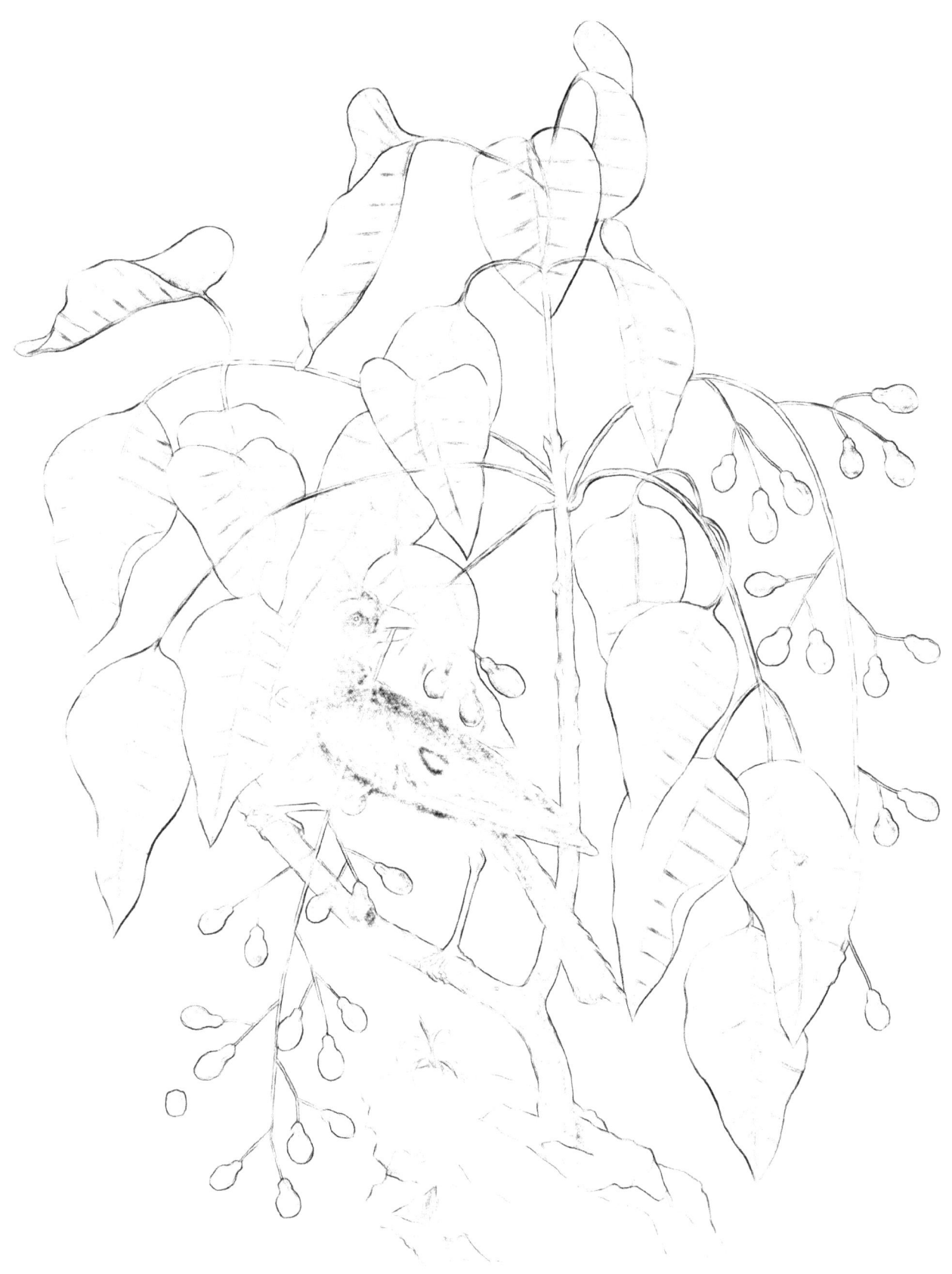

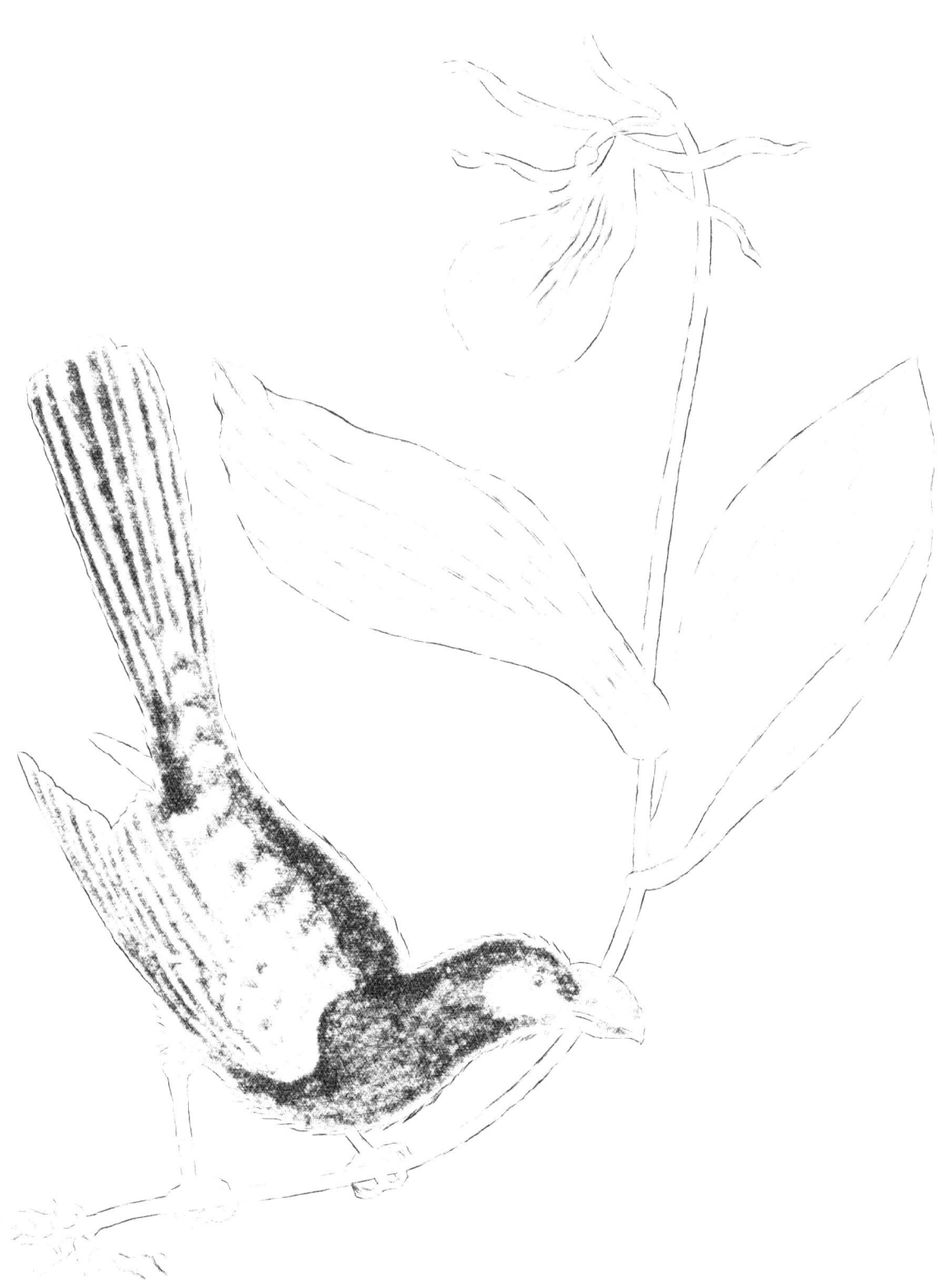

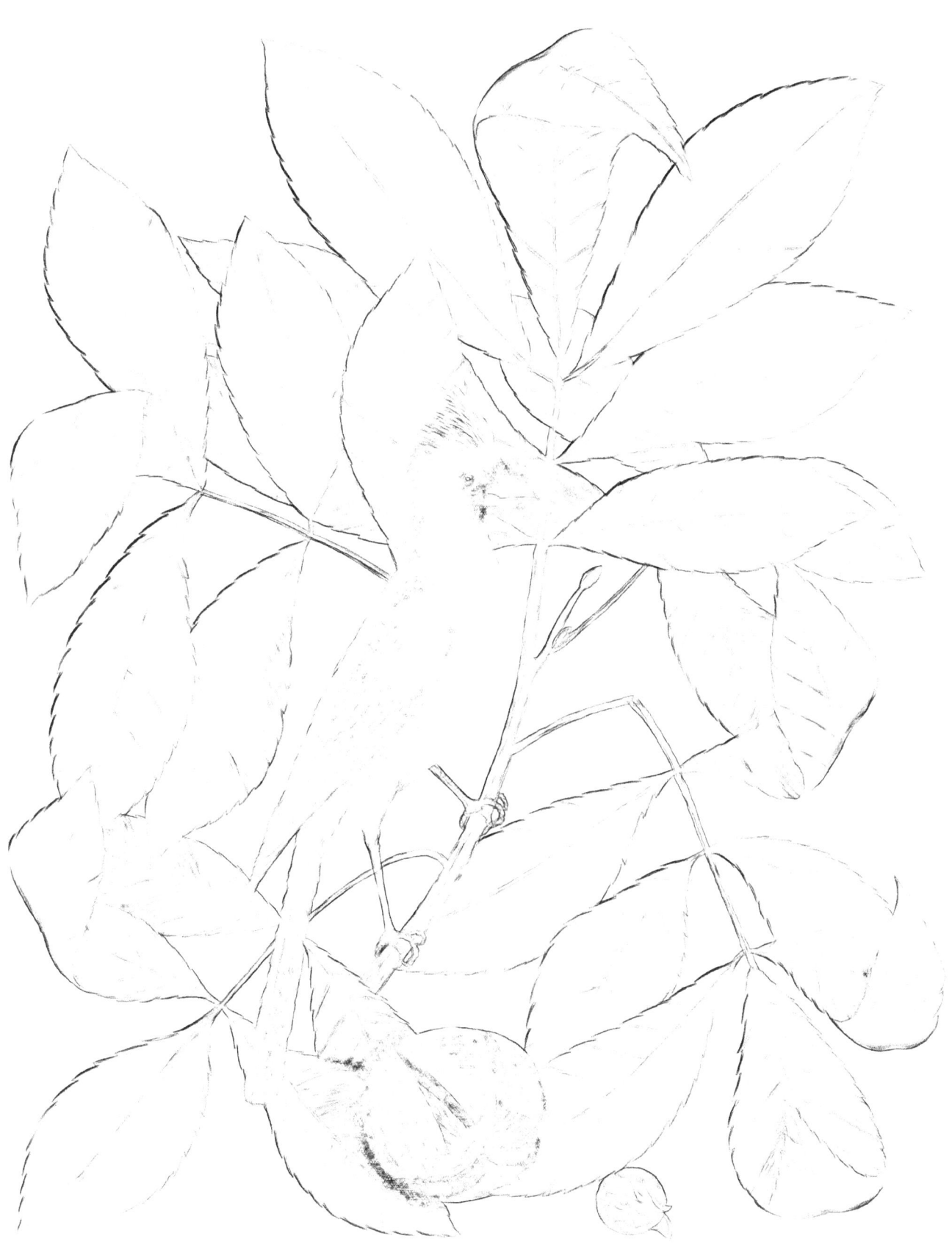

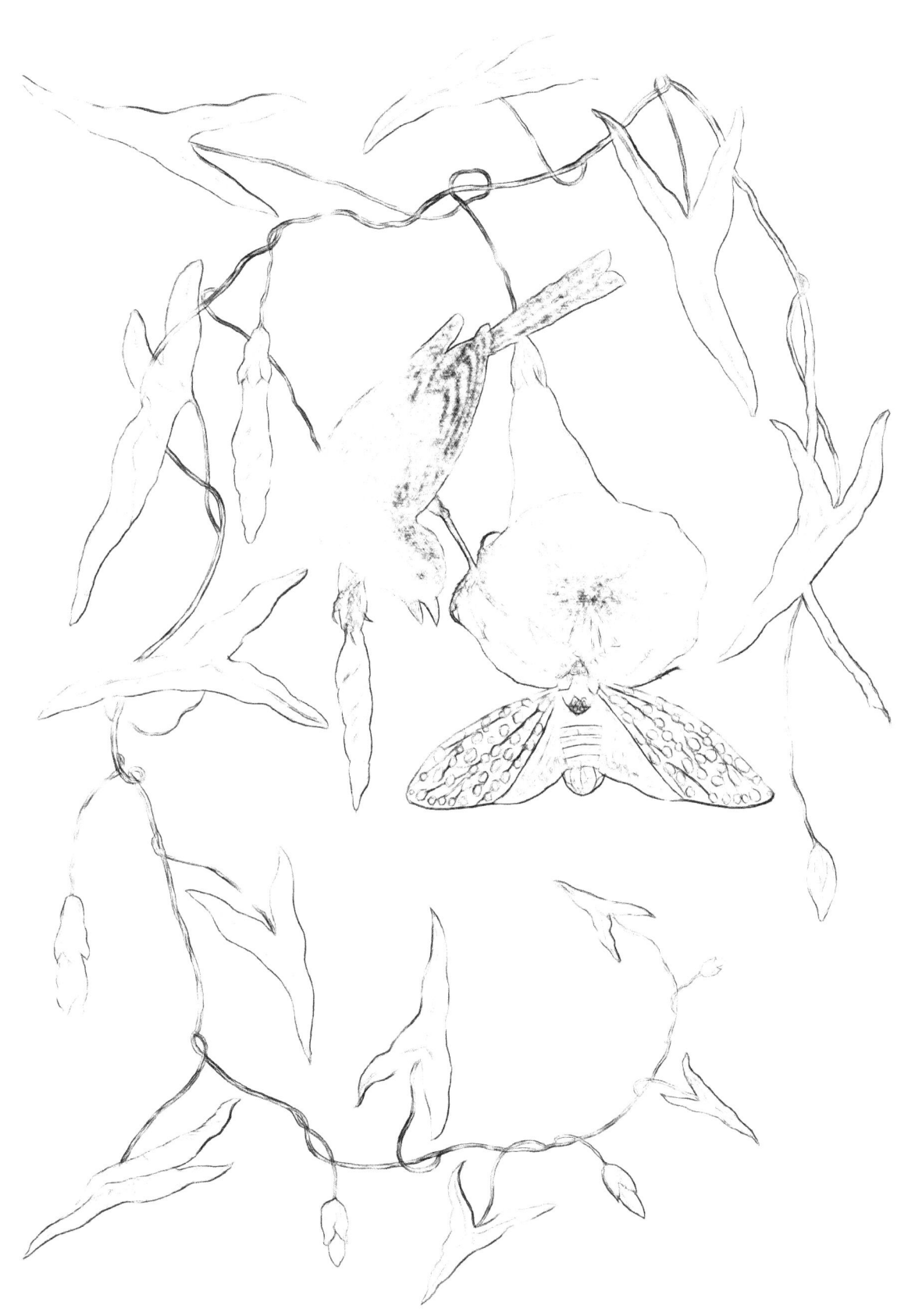

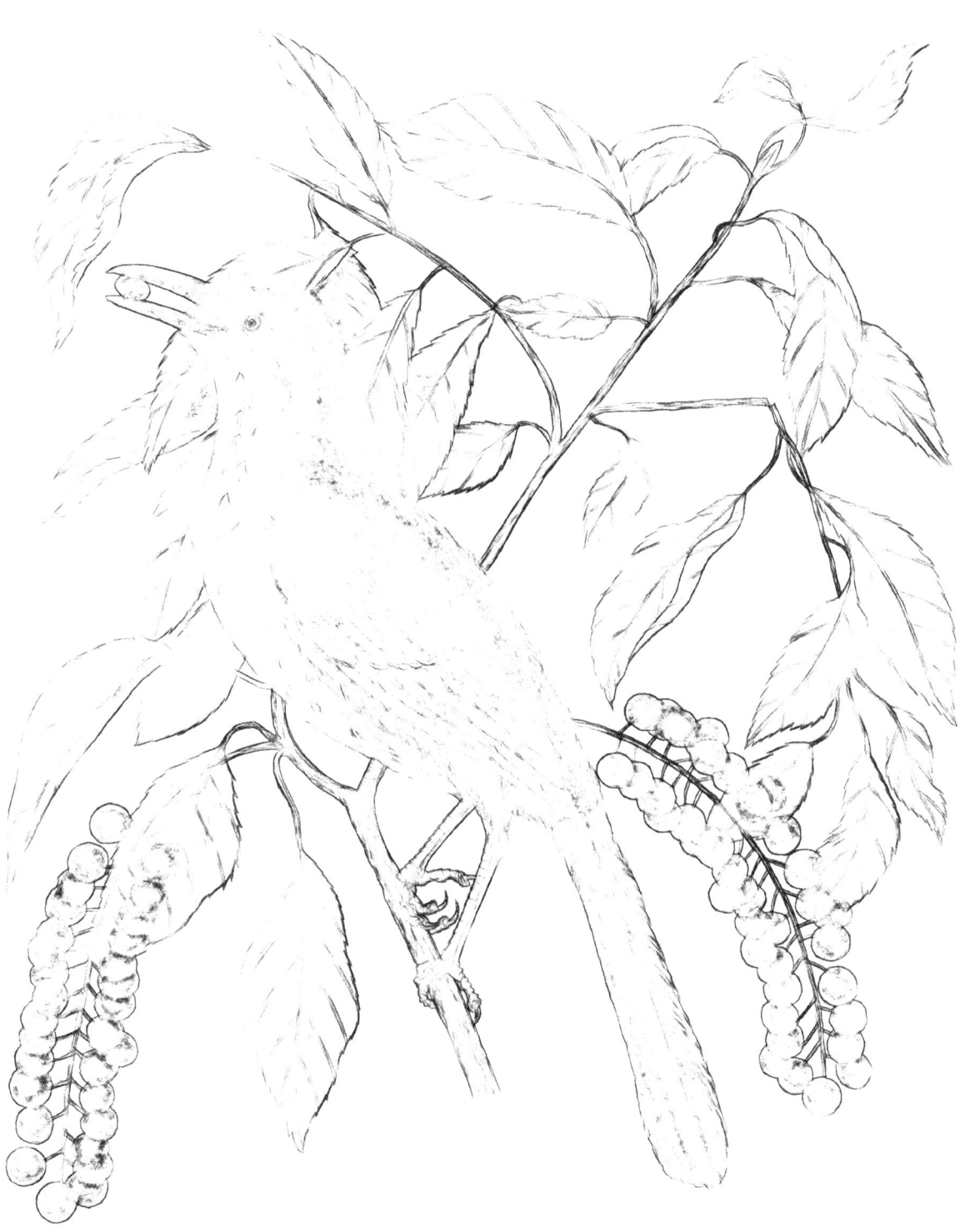

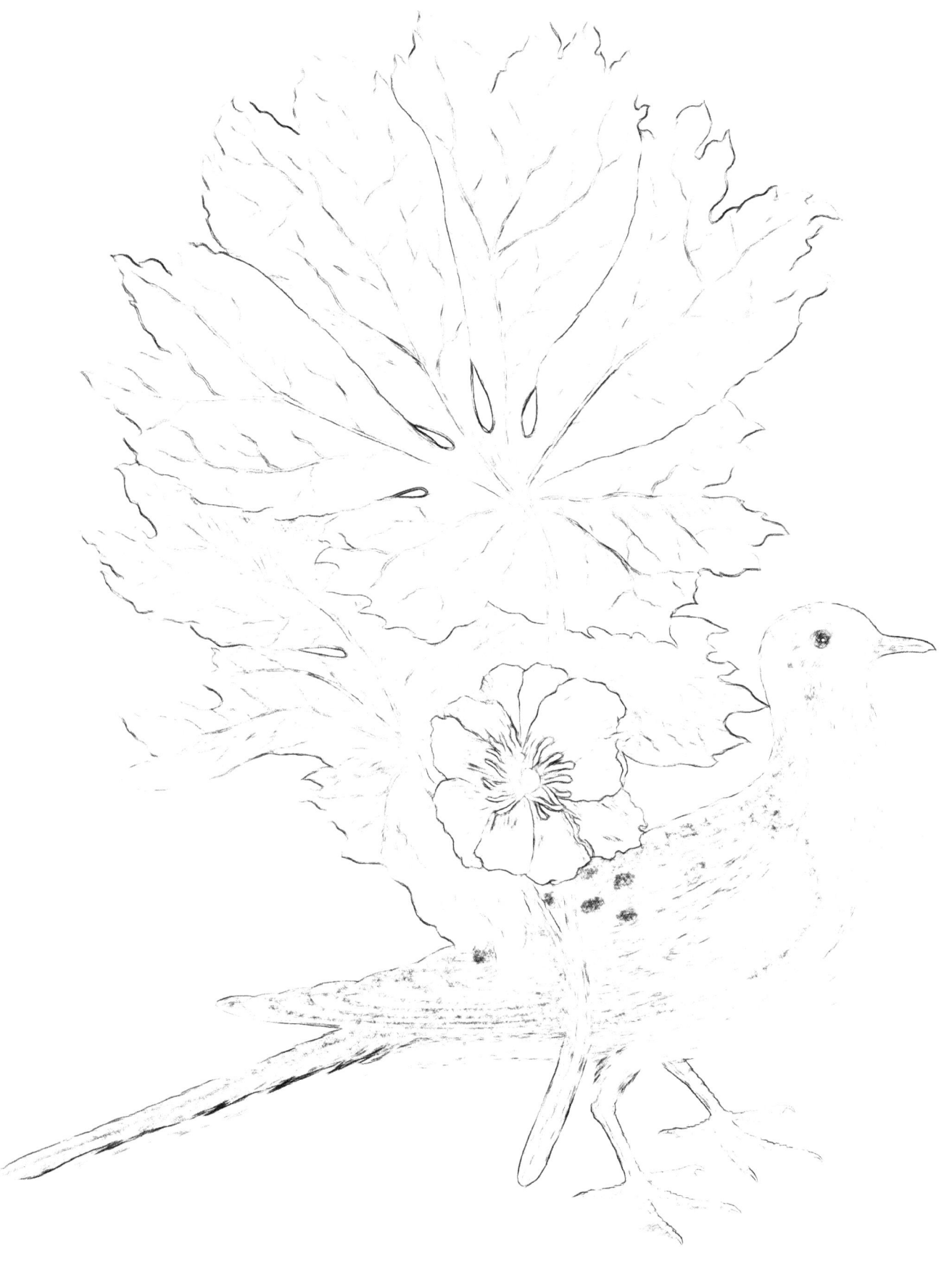

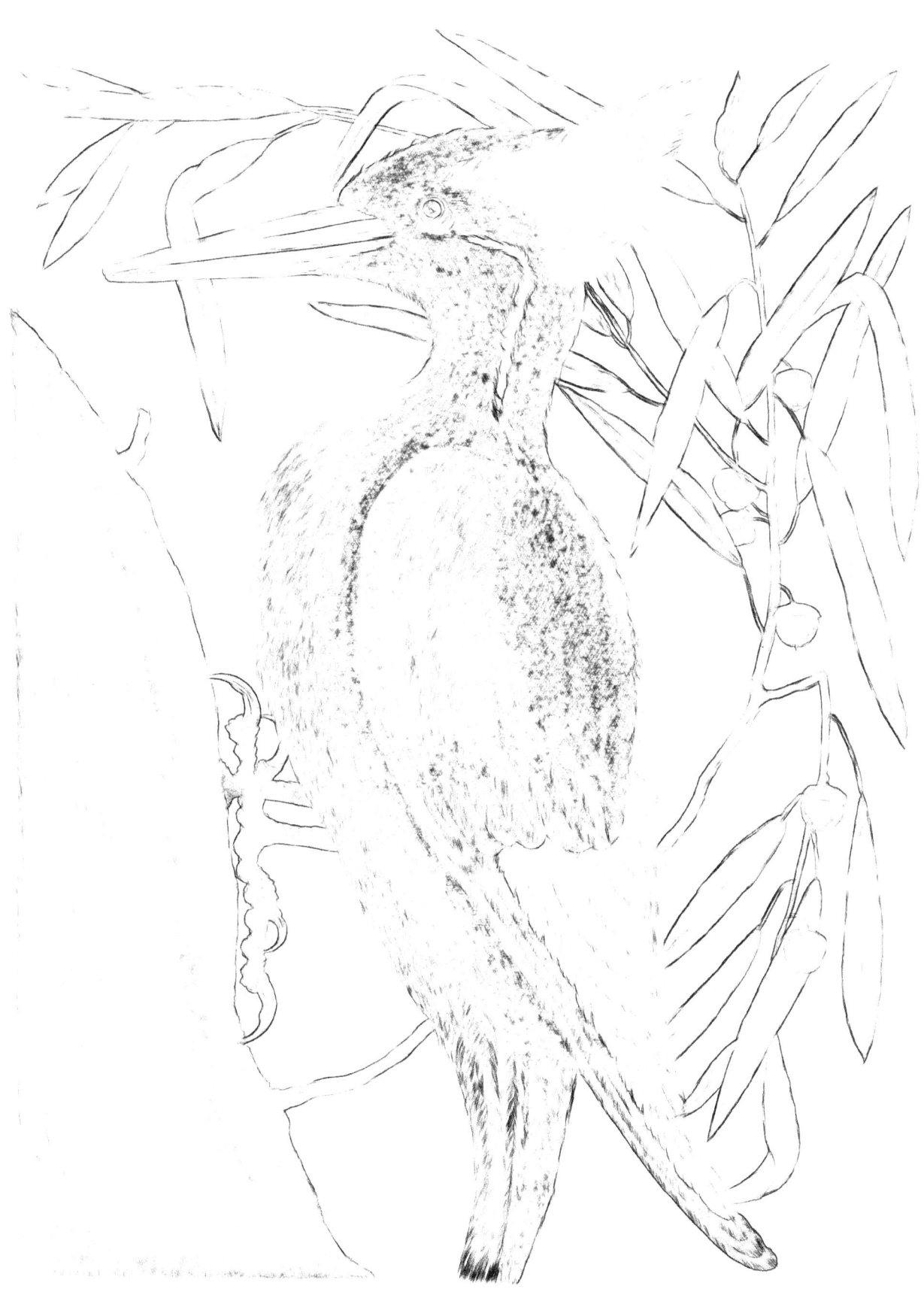

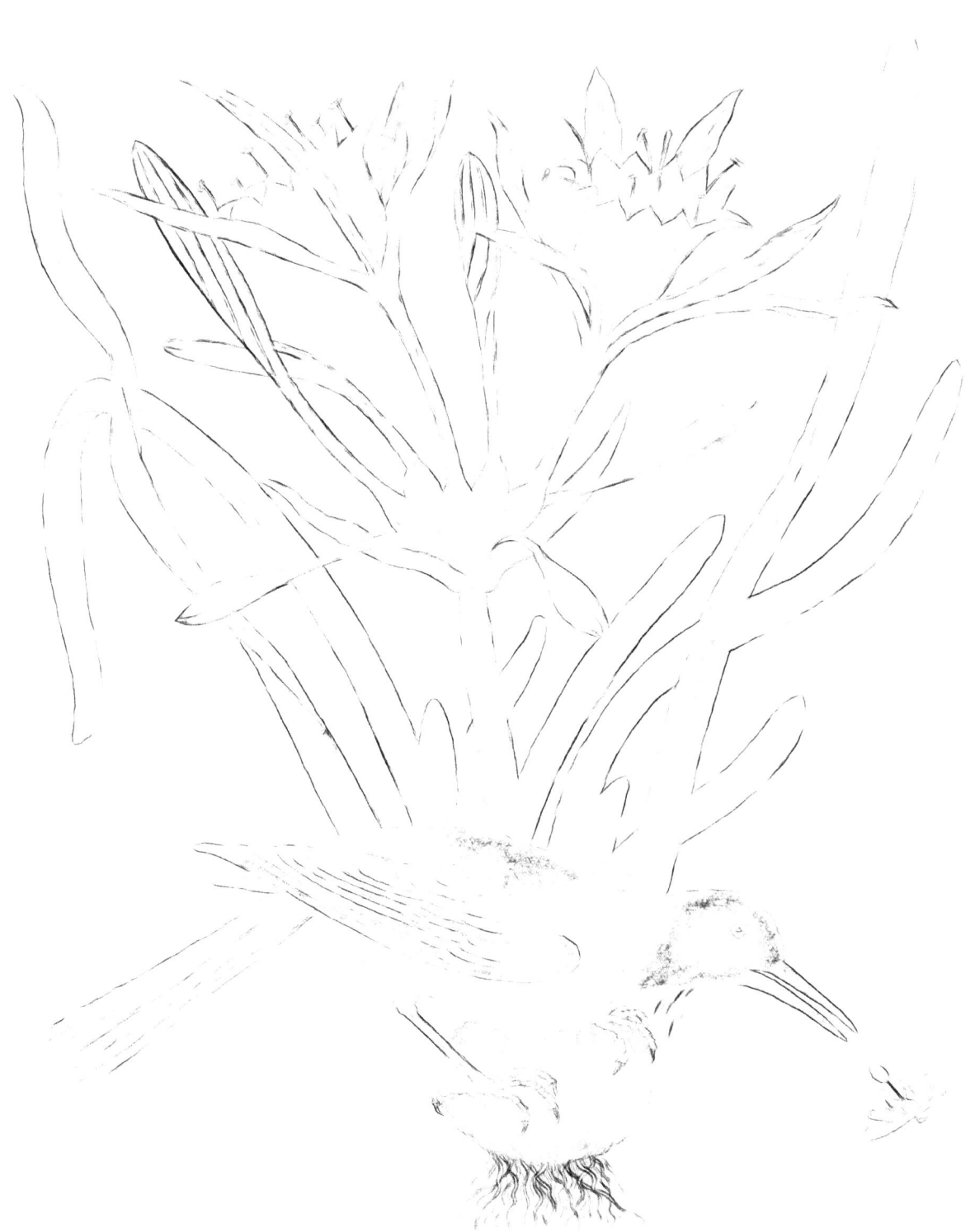

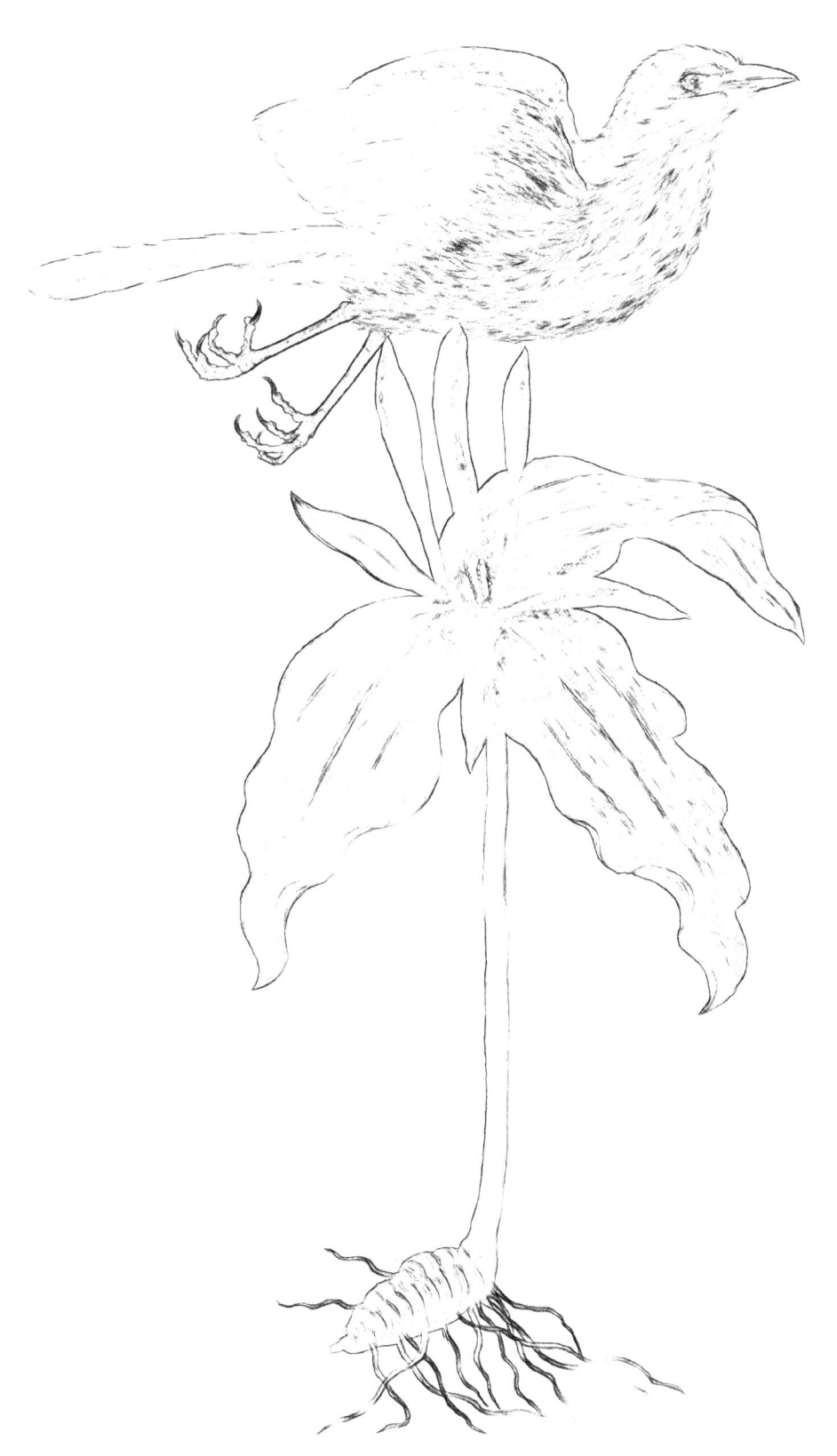

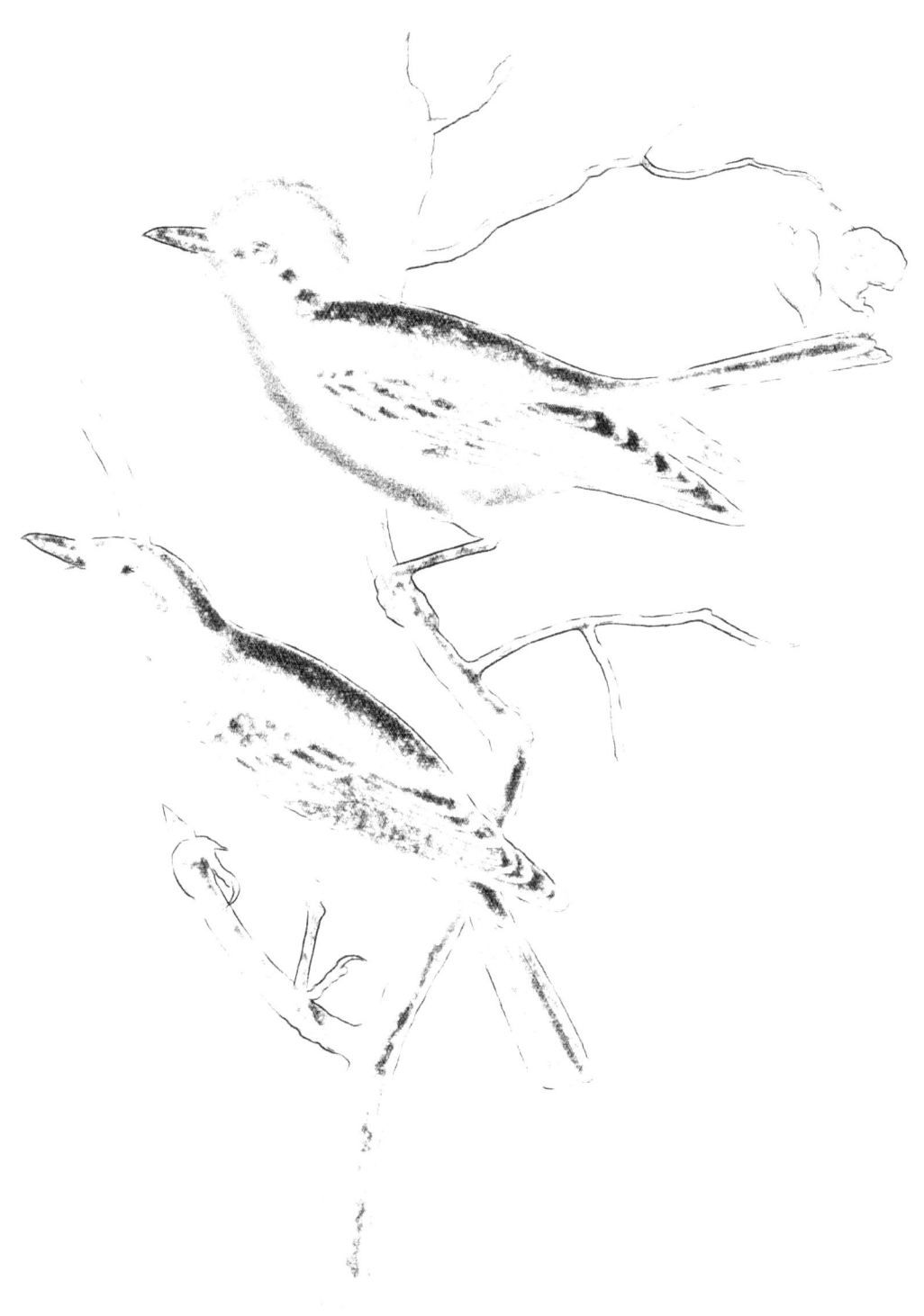